AF230757

GRAPHOLOGIES

Phil Cohen
with Jean McNeil

Mica Press

d

This book is dedicated to the memory of our beloved son, Stephen.

Published in the United Kingdom in 2014 by
Leslie Bell trading as Mica Press
47 Belle Vue Road
Wivenhoe
Colchester
Essex
CO7 9LD

ISBN 978-1-869848-02-6
First Edition

FOREWORD AND ACKNOWLEDGEMENTS

This book is a hybrid text, the fruit of a partnership over many years between a poet/ethnographer and a painter who have mutually enriched each other's understanding of the meaning of place. The book takes a line of thought for a walk across poetry, the visual arts, autobiography and fiction, exploring the hidden emotional and narrative hinterlands of the commonplace.

We are grateful to Denise Riley and Carole Satyamurti for their very helpful suggestions for improving the text and for their general encouragement.

Some of the poems first appeared in Soundings, Agenda, Critical Quarterly, Kites and Words Down the Line.

As we were completing this manuscript we were devastated by the death of our adopted son, Stephen, who shared with us many moments of entrancement with the land and seascapes depicted here. The memory of his presence will continue to inspire our work.

We would like to thank Leslie Bell for his kindness and generosity of purpose in steering the book through the production stages and for designing the cover, and Kate Nevard for proof-reading.

Our greatest debt is to each other.

Phil Cohen and Jean McNeil
Wivenhoe, January - June 2014

h

CONTENTS

Foreword and acknowledgements

Introduction   page 1

One: Neither Prospect nor Refuge   page 9

Lullabies for a War Baby - Night Walk - Fallout - Winter Gloves -
Love Poem - Triptych for Lorca - Chorograph - Parting Shots -
Living in Time - Diagnostic - Doctor's Orders - A Short Counter-history of
Poetics

Two: Birthplaces   page 33

Home Alone - Siren Call - Cold Comfort Farm - Birthday Suit -
Bedtime Story - Oceanic Feeling - Utility Chairs - Under the Concrete, the
Beach - Vice Versa - Growing Pains

Three: Like as Not: excerpts from Arnold K's memoir   page 41

Editorial Note - Baptismal Naming - Trade Mark - The Tower of Babel -
The City of Déjà Vu - The Executor - Blood Wedding - Milan's Narrative -
Like as Not: the Voyage - Diary Entry - Coroner's Report - Notes

List of Images   page 76

About the authors   page 78

INTRODUCTION

Maps and territories

He had brought a large map
Representing the sea,
Without the least vestige of land:
And the crew were much pleased
When they found it to be
A map they could all understand.

- Lewis Carroll, The Hunting of the Snark

Lewis Carroll's map is described as an 'ocean chart' and it is entirely blank. Around its borders are inscribed a series of nautical and geographical terms: Zenith, Longitude, Nadir, North Pole, West, Meridian, Torrid Zone, Equator, etc, in a quite nonsensical order, bearing no relation to their spatial location or function on any real map of the world. Carroll is making an elaborate joke at the expense of official cartography, but he is also saying something quite profound about the arbitrary nature of the relation, and sometimes the non-relation, between map and territory.

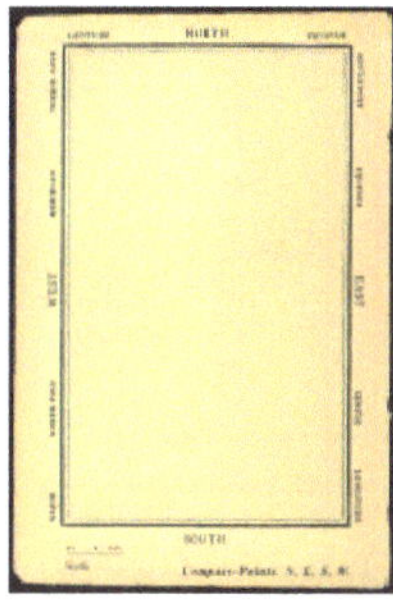

When the philosopher Alfred Korzybski made his famous remark that 'the map is not the territory,' he was trying to draw attention to the discrepancy that exists between the world as revealed by science and how it is imagined to be in common sense and also by artists. Korzybski was concerned about the consequences of the widening gap between the languages of science, art and everyday vernacular, which he saw as a source of potential confusion about the relation between word and world. The word 'sugar' is not itself sweet, and, we might add, in view of its material history as a commodity connected historically to the slave trade, and its negative impact on health, it may leave quite a bitter taste in the mouth, even if this is unlikely to stop people from eating it. Map and territory can easily become dissociated. There is much in contemporary philosophy and aesthetics which insists,

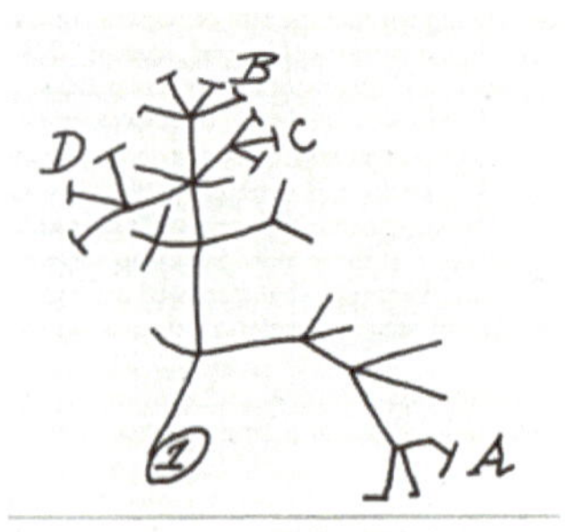

Charles Darwin (1837)

with Jean Baudrillard, that 'the territory no longer precedes the map, nor does it survive it, rather the map precedes the territory and engenders the territory'. Those who dwell in such abstractions, who cannot see the trees for the wood, are unlikely to recognise the challenge of comprehending the particularities of experience within some wider scheme of things without reducing them to symptomatic or generic effects.

We may yearn for some absolute, guaranteed, one-to-one correspondence between map and territory but we also secretly know that it is not possible and if it was, there would be no need for poetry, dreams or art. The pathetic fallacy and the fallacy of misplaced concreteness both testify to the traps which magically collapsing the gap in scope and scale produces. In *Sylvie and Bruno* Lewis Carroll features a fictional map that has the scale of a mile to the mile and one of his characters notes the practical difficulties this entails: "we now use the country itself, as its own map, and I assure you it does nearly as well."

Taking more than a leaf out of Carroll's book, J-L Borges pushes the notion of correspondence to a reductio ad absurdum : 'Let us imagine that a portion of the soil of England has been levelled off perfectly and that on it a cartographer traces a map of England. The job is perfect; there is no detail of the soil of England, no matter how minute, that is not registered on the map; everything has there its correspondence. This map, in such a case, should contain a map of the map, which should contain a map of the map of the map, and so on to infinity'.

Against this background, our starting point is that map and territory do not exist independently of one another, closed off in separate domains, but rather are present in and through particular patterns of their inter-animation. It is these patterns, these fragile bridges between the mental maps we construct about the world in order to classify and organise it, and that more embodied sense of space and time we create as we navigate and weave stories around the places we come to inhabit, name and claim, which have fascinated poets and painters, cultural geographers and ethnographers, and which form the subject matter of this book. Images and texts, poems and prose, facts and fictions, the imaginative and the analytic, are here brought together in order to explore the implications of the *lack* of correspondence between map and territory for the ways objects and subjects, lives and landscapes, can be imagined and represented.

Across these different idioms the book is concerned to depict moments of disorientation or disjuncture, in which the taken-for-granted nature of the world becomes suddenly problematic and its peculiarity, its sheer 'as-iffiness' comes into focus. This may occur as a result of some more or less brutal and unexpected disruption to everyday routine, for example through the advent of war or illness, bereavement, or some other personal calamity; it may happen whenever we visit a foreign country, or find ourselves in an unfamiliar part of town. When and wherever we suddenly feel at a loss.

It is when and where the common place and our traffic with it can no longer be taken for granted that we are both tempted to fall back on familiar linguistic devices - clichés - to 'normalise' the situation; but it is precisely at this point we have the opportunity to reach for new forms of expression that register more accurately this unsettling of accounts. Lewis Carroll's 'Ocean Chart' achieves this effect by a deliberate act of disorientation. When landlubbers look out to sea, all they observe is a vast undifferentiated expanse of nothing, a blank sheet of paper on which to write their fear of the unknown. For mariners, in contrast, the sea is densely populated with topographical features. Every sandbank, every channel has its name and with that name a history. The working knowledge of particular coastlines, their tidal and navigational idiosyncrasies, becomes embedded in a narrative whose co-ordinates are as precise as longitude and latitude and just as indispensable. A study of fishermen from the Farne Islands showed that they had a complex network of stories, information and personal

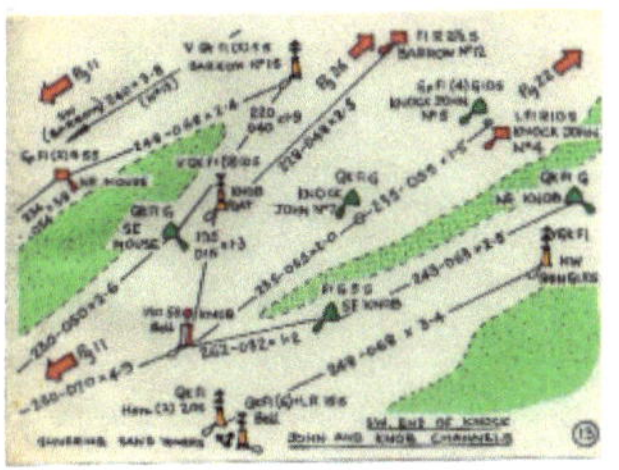

reference, identified not by date but by the personal events with which they were associated, and which they used to help identify specific locations in the fishing grounds: 'We shot 5,000 mussel-baited hooks here and got 133 stones of haddocks the day Jimmy Stephenson's Mam and Dad were married'.

With the advent of GPS, the sea, like the city, has become de-territorialised and its locally situated knowledge officially declared redundant. In principle you no longer need to study the terrain or learn how to read a map, just input the co-ordinates of your chosen waypoints and the satnav will tell you how to get there. In practice it is somewhat a different story as evidenced by all those whose journeys, or lives, refuse to unfold according to the plan view. It is because the gap between map and territory cannot be bridged by prosthetic technologies or gazetteers that its presence is so strongly registered and plotted on a more personal atlas.

This gap belongs to what Freud called 'the other scenes' of everyday life, where what has been repressed or pushed to the margins of consciousness returns, often in a coded form, to disturb the commonplace and haunt the imagination. Poets and ethnographers are both in their different ways acutely sensitised to this phenomenon. They both use techniques of 'de-familiarisation' to render what is familiar, strange, and translate what is strange or ignored, into more accessible forms. They both adopt a standpoint or strategy of observation that rests on what has been termed 'legitimate peripheral participation', being fully part of but never wholly immersed in the world, alert to its emergent properties without surrendering to their seductive appeal. This is perhaps why both kinds of observation are fascinated by liminality and transience, the edgy spaces and disjointed times where worlds may be turned upside down and monsters lurk; to enter this zone requires a special rite of passage, an apprenticeship to the frailty of the human condition which includes a method for fully registering its effects without being overwhelmed by them.

Wallace Stevens developed a whole poetics around this sensibility. He wrote:

From this the poem springs: that we live in a place
That is not our own and, much more, not ourselves

Stevens has the counter-intuitive insight that the poem is fashioned less by conscious design or intent than by what escapes any attempt to capture or pin down its special occasion: its other scene. By the same token its meaning cannot be reduced to the social circumstances of its production, and this closely parallels a concept of culture as an arbitrary and unconscious process which anthropologists hold to, and which has been richly documented by ethnographers. Such a perspective was, for example, an essential part of the initial programme of Mass Observation in the 1930's. It is no coincidence that MO's founding spirits, Charles Madge and Humphrey Jennings, were, respectively, a poet and painter, as well as sociologists; they were interested in investigating what Lautréamont called ' the poetry made by all' or, as they put it, 'the shouts and gestures of motorists; the aspidistra cult; the anthropology of football pools; bathroom behaviour; beards, armpits and eyebrows; the distribution, diffusion and significance of the dirty joke'.

Ethno-Graphologies

A major point of connection between poetry and ethnography is a shared concern with the particular and the concrete, as against the generic and abstract. Both disciplines are committed to 'thick description', to showing rather than just telling. It is this graphic dimension which gives them an elective affinity to the mimetic arts of drawing, painting and photography. We are still used to thinking that these media are about capturing presence, and/or copying external reality in order to master it. But they are as much if not more about absence and its representation. In the classical myth elaborated by Pliny, drawing begins life as a means of preserving and protecting an object of affection that is about to be lost: a Corinthian girl traces the shadow of her lover on a wall when he is about to go on a long journey. She draws his contour by retreating from his presence into a shadowy space and it is in and from this 'place that is not herself' that she casts a spell in which loss is allayed; the fact of absence is countered by the process of bringing an image into being which is the cry of its occasion and serves as its remembrance. The photograph operates a similar magic, though it conjures up absence-as-presence through quite different means: it allows an object to be drawn in light, through the camera lens, onto paper or screen; a transient moment of time is frozen, a fragmentary space consolidated in a graphic detail, so that it can be invested with a special evidential or sentimental claim on our attention.

'Graphology' in the sense in which it is used here has nothing to do with attempts to read personality traits from someone's hand writing. Rather it points to the 'graphic' as a specific domain of expression which exists between the trace and the sign, the model and the metaphor, and whose poetics cannot be reduced either to the scopic or the textual, even though these more dominant forms continually encroach on its practice. The root meaning of 'graph' is to represent something by means of a line; whether the line in question is created by the methods of poetry or drawing, whether it belongs to the co-ordinates of a map or theory, or the special narrative framing generated by a photograph, it creates an aura of distance or liminality around what it depicts, even as it fixes the meaning or value that can be attached to it. In this book images are used to demonstrate this uncanny graphology while the texts, in their varying idioms, set out to articulate its different modalities. In bringing these images and texts together within the same frame, our aim has been to give uncommon places a local habitation and a name, in Italo Calvino's words ' to find within the inferno, that which is not inferno, and give it space, make it endure'.

The seascape and its depiction is perhaps the most enduring challenge. Seen from the shore the eye is inevitably lured to the horizon, to some fixed point of reference, to get its bearings, but once there has nothing further to observe. But that is not the end of the story. For some the seascape beckons adventure, for others the horror of shipwreck, but in either case it disturbs our common sense of scope and scale. We can easily find ourselves out of our depth and as Stevie Smith famously put it 'not waving but drowning'. Once we are no longer harboured by the land, once we are fully at sea, we have to find other principles of navigation. In a large ship we view the sea from a safe platform as a spectacle of nature, but in a small boat in rough weather each wave is a close up of vaster elements that defy such easy representation. Taking a line of thought or feeling for a walk, as a point moving forward in the midst of such turbulence, means keeping a space open between the foreclosures of both the prospect and the refuge. Finding and sustaining that ever shifting point of balance is what the work here recorded is all about.

Sea Wall with Figures

The first part of the book contains a series of poems and paintings that explore the hinterland of the commonplace across a range of idioms and genres. There are love poems, narrative poems, poems about separation and loss and poems occasioned by the impress of landscapes and seascapes linked to particular encounters and events. The paintings by Jean McNeil invoke a sense of transient things arrested in the moment of their manifestation or imminent departure: a tide that is on the turn, a glimpse of a landscape from a train, a passing storm.... She is attracted to elements of strangeness in these familiar scenes: an unusual light, surprising arrangements of shapes. These effects are sometimes heightened by the process of recording the scene in a photograph: the colours may be distorted, the shapes fixed by the frame may suggest a composition which can be taken further in the studio.

The standpoint of lyric poetry and romantic painting is here explicitly rejected, even and especially where the work deliberately occupies that terrain. These words and images offer neither a world bounded by secure horizons, nor a space and time of emotion reflected in tranquillity. They aim neither for the picturesque or the sublime. Instead they explore the edgelands of experience, the space between the commanding view offered by the panorama, and the resting point for the weary breath or eye provided by the easy line break or figure/ground relation. The resolution or homecoming on offer here is one which retains the sense of ambiguity, evanescence or uncanniness that prompted the composition in the first place.

The sometimes hidden, sometimes explicit reference point for much of this work is the East Anglian countryside and coast where we have both lived over the past twenty years, providing a local habitation and a name for our various preoccupations with the hidden liminalities of the commonplace.

Perhaps we should stress that in no way are the poems and paintings directly related to each other. The poems were not written as a direct response to a particular painting nor was a particular painting directly inspired or done to illustrate a particular poem. They have been matched in retrospect either because they seem to be exploring the same terrain of feeling, because they counterpoint or supplement one another or there is some thematic link.

Fictive concords

We all create personal myths of origin, and in many of them, particularly those fictional genealogies that Freud called the family romance, we re-invent ourselves as the offspring of famous people, living in faraway exotic places as a means to both distance ourselves from our actual parents and cling on to an idealised version of who we would like them to be. As we grow up these first memoryscapes, in which the real and imagined are merged, continue to haunt our sense of the present and future, even as they turn our past into a foreign country whose language we no longer speak and whose customs come to seem bizarre.

The desire to return to these birthplaces of the imagination is fertile ground for both writers and artists. The second part of the book consists of a series of short prose pieces exploring the memoryscape of a childhood in which intimate spaces of fear and delight become refracted through the trauma of the London Blitz.

The final part of the book takes the form of a fictional memoir featuring the mysterious K, who might just be a refugee from The Castle or a close relative of Brecht's Mr Keuner. The eponymous hero, Arnold Kvaktum, recalls a journey of self-discovery as he explores the surreal landscape of his childhood and youth growing up in a dystopian society of the future where 'soapspeak' and 'knowgov' are the only permitted discourses. The pervasive sense of personal dislocation, of a lack of concordance between the officially authorised map and the unfolding territory of a life, here results in a series of phantasmagoric events culminating in a suicidal sea voyage. The photographs which accompany the text anchor the narrative to its 'other scene'.

In moving across these various media, from poems to prose, from text to image, from the singularities of experience to the peculiarities of historical circumstance, and between the imaginary, the symbolic and the real, the reader is invited to consult their own sense of what renders common places less so.

ONE: NEITHER PROSPECT NOR REFUGE

The poem is the cry of its occasion,
Part of the thing itself and not about it

– Wallace Stevens

LULLABIES FOR A WAR BABY

One

Every night, sirens sang you to sleep
Like alley cats howling for the moon.
When the big burps started,
We picked you up and ran for cover.
Down in the shelter, Gran iced a flying bomb
For your birthday.
Once exiled on her stony lap
You blew out both the candles in your head
And left yourself for dead.

Two

'Better to spit out the truth than swallow lies'
You snarl, in one of the voices you use
To break the silent suffocating siege. I laugh
Lips open as if for food, your words
Flying fish caught in mid air
As I come up gasping out of the locked depths.
Landing at last on a warm shore.
I turn my head, breathe in, breathe out,
'The coast is clear' I almost shout.

NIGHT WALK

Look there, she said,
A giant has blown a smoke ring
In the sky, a halo
For the harvest moon.
I earthed her gaze to mine,
Down to a lunar landscape nearer home:
Fields phosphorous with pebbles
From another shore,
Cows steaming in the cold night air.
Hidden in woods
Pheasants go off like firecrackers
As we walk on, not speaking,
Seeking the missing element
To make the circuit of our walk
Complete.

Wild Wood

FALLOUT

Most lie against railings
Or underfoot, heaped up
Anticipating
The twisted shape of death,
Kick starting memories
Of another war
When bonfires spiced the air
With promises of requiem.

Elsewhere a few survivors
Of the genocidal gales
Murmur no regrets
For the cremation of summer
With its mass foliations,
The strange burden of shade.

There will be no easy falling
To rest this year, no pressing
Between the pages
Of some familiar archive;
Each leaf is hand picked
Out of the wind's grasp,
Pored over, like a precious map
For traces of a Life to come.

If there are secrets weathered in these veins
They are not ours to read.
Better to trust the slow compost
Of unearthed roots,
The burrow of Old Mole
Blindly scenting home.

Autumn Bonfire

WINTER GLOVES

They came wrapped in the promise
of snowballs and perfect partnership
but it did not snow that year,
the season's swaddling of touch
no match for the treachery of growth,
the slow ungloving of appetite,
and then came Spring.

Holding hands long coddled
from the elements, we cut off our finger tips
and learnt to grope for pocketfuls of danger
amidst the ruins of Winter. One day
I found a lone survivor of the season's cull
lying like a broken wing on playground railings
and brought it home for knitting into myth.

My first design was for a phantom fist,
cut off from its spar and angry for asylum,
demanding the office of Lost Property;
my second drew cuckoo fingers
feeling for flaws and fledgling hates
to nest a story.

The legerdemain that children know
I had to find elsewhere; if not in you
then the gift you wrapped my coldness in;
if not the instant fit, the slow wearing into shape;
if not the thing itself, the game of hide and seek
we made of it. So many quiet impressments
of your love in mine.

From the Train, Snow

LOVE POEM

One morning, rushing to work
Through a corridor of house plants
Whose names you tell me
But I always forget -
Except the geranium
Whose scent is touched off
By every brush with it -
I find your note
Stuck to a small shrub:
Please be careful
It may not look like anything
But it's a baby.

Later, on the train,
I smell my fingers,
Still geranium through the soil
Of the day's traffic,
And remember
Your shy movements
Of care, the deft arrangement
Of local features, making home,
The canvas primed
With infant landscapes
Tensed against storms.

When my world grows dark
And angry, you teach me
How to spell the chance
Of better weather, eyes widening
Then blinking shut, quick as a cat's
And just as much a sign of trust
In the Old Mole, burrowing up
From under sheeted fields
To get a sniff of sea spray
in Penelope's hair.

Waking together, early,
We fall off the edge
Of precipitous dreams
Into a Castilian garden.
You paint the singing leaves,
I grub about the undergrowth
Looking for the notes
You planted in me long ago.
It may not look like anything,
This small stub of a poem,
But be careful with it :
It is my love, growing.

Spring Trees

TRIPTYCH FOR LORCA

Lanjarón

On the dusty promenade
the old couple move slowly

between fountain and almond tree
almond tree and fountain

waiting for news
of summer's end.

Barrio Hondillo

Little fountain of Hondillo
what is your Madonna dreaming of ?

Is she flying up the mountain
on the back of some young man's motorbike?

or is she floating in your arms,
thinking of the Passion still to come?

Ulysses in translation

On the beach at El Peño
where once Phoenicians and Moriscos danced
he works the line of parasols

around his head a halo
of tobacco smoke, in his hair
canaries flutter and glint

on his chest the sign reads
God Is Great. On his back
a map of Africa proclaims:

the future is closer than you think.

CHOROGRAPH

An instrument designed to determine the position of a hidden spot given the angles made to it by three points in the same plane, whose positions are already known.

One

In the gap, just wide enough
For two horses to pass
The bridle path squeezed
Between caravans and wheat field,
Pursuing its lonely traffic
With the sea.
Wordlessly, I lose the track
In a confusion of dunes
Where steel warps rear up
Like giant brambles
Out of the scoured clay,
As if warding off the waves
Of metal detectors
That wash over the beach
In daily search of treasure
Buried in the ruins
Of ancient sandcastles.

Two

Up on the cliff top, local lads
Wise in the art of collecting
History's small change
Comb through the marram grass
For offertory coins, dropped by the faithful
Fleeing God's wrath
'that terrible winter's night of 1898'
When the Devil's own floodtide
Churned the church to pebble dash.

Three

In the broken shadow of the lighthouse
(restored courtesy Dulux PLC)
Sunday poets congregate
Pencil sharp and eager
To glean a last harvest song
From the village carter
Before he sinks into the wind blurred
lie of the land.

Somewhere along the way
Between then and now
Worked field turned into playground
Fallow became vacant lot
Memory, souvenir.
Searching for a point of balance
I stumble on the path's own stillness
Notice a gap in the hedgerow
And a pigeon resting there
Half dead from the labour
Of flight across oceans
And the news she carries
Of waves that do not break on any shore.

Dazzle

PARTING SHOTS

"Stephen, learning to windsurf
Norfolk Broads, August 1993"

The caption pins our hope to his,
for an instant lets us hold his thin body
between finger, thumb and sky,
measuring how far he's come
before he wriggles free, cocooned
in black rubber, making his own way.

No chance to smooth the scowl,
he holds the pose he wants,
tense and sombre against the flaming sail,
daring us to walk on water, daring us to fail.

Remember his face fisting the wind,
the sudden keeling over like a heart attack,
our throwaway safety lines:
"Keep going, hold on, that's it, well done!"
Each grab at mastery, a flash back
of that first defeated struggle
to come out on top, knowing that you're not.

The echoes of what had to be adopted
to reach a point of balance, wash back,
like secret tidings, stirring hidden elements to life.
The wind frets at the waves
whipping up ancient fears
of defences flooded,
being drowned in dreams.
There was no sudden giving up
only a slow whittling away of what bound us
to a common hope. Now it is too late
he can be picked up, held in the mind's eye,
lightweight as a snapshot, fickle as a sigh.

"Norfolk Broads, Summer, 1994".
Words wrap round absence
like cling film sealing in the hurt.
Easier to look away or change the frame,
a yacht with a black sail parts the mist,
a painting or a post card to an old school friend:
"Having a quiet and restful time,
so far no rain."

Passing Storm

LIVING IN TIME

For Phil Salmon

'I am sorry there is no one here to take your call'...
her voice is poignant, unmistakable;
this is no official announcement of regret
but eloquent of other sadnesses
she would not burden callers with.

Those who did call on her
as mentor, teacher, friend
know how little time she had
for fake observances,
scoring academic points.

She spoke her mind,
writing a special kind of poetry
not measured in metre
but in careful cadences
of hard won truth.

In an age of mechanical induction
she drew on memory to teach
the proper usages of grief,
how not to make our grievances
a method of instruction.

She taught us that education
is not business, bureaucracy,
or a football league,
it is where the generations meet
on treacherous uneven ground
often at cross purposes, driven
by fear of failure suddenly revealed
in frantic games of leap frog
over never levelled playing fields
to reach the future first.

Standing there, observing life at school,
she notes the awkward teenager she once was:
the one in the end-of-term photograph
with the troubled smile, finding herself
trapped in the lens's public glare
exposed to the gaze
of people who would never know
or care about her private agonies,
the work she had to do,
just being there, on show.

The endgame was no different.
She held her camera lucida
steady, unafraid to look
Mistress Palsy full in the face
and call her bluff ; when others
would have given in
to pity's subtle flattery,
she was made of sterner stuff.

Her style was plain song
not baroque; an elegiac
counterpoint to death's
slow march. Disowning
pre-recorded messages
of shock we hear her voice
ring out again: 'please speak clearly
when you hear the tone'.

No need for grace notes, then,
or flowery tributes; no canned
condolences or choirs,
no churchiness without the spires.
Instead, let us renew her story
as we mourn her loss.
Be angry for her
that the days drew in so fast;

hope that endorphin angels
took away the pain, but left her dreams
intact; be glad at being so apprenticed
to her craft, of learning
how to live in time.

Path to the Woods

DIAGNOSTIC

How well pain
educated her body
to its subtle plan,
tissue and bone
tightened around the Cactus
growing in her spine.

Prostrate she waits
for Lady Sciatica
to start the dance,
each step wired
to the shock machine,
pulse on pulse of rage.

Cocooned in illness
beyond the reach
of pills, her plaints
grew monstrous,
thick with triumphs
scored against the world.

Now, in my turn
upon the wrack,
I learn the subtle art
of self-deception
scrupulously, at last,
my mother's son.

Light Flaw

DOCTOR'S ORDERS

You see this bowl
with blue and orange flowers?
It was her favourite.
Wash away the blood streaked sputum
in rivers she never swam across,
dry with bunches of hair
she lost to the drugs,
wrap in the tartan scarf
she wore that last summer,
and place, like a charm,
under her empty bed
so she may get some rest
from the cough that barked at the moon
night
after night
after night.

A SHORT COUNTER-HISTORY OF POETICS

How unbecoming a poet
To use a toothpick, not a dictionary
To find the gristle of meaning
In a sausage, as it lies, so raw
And indigestible on the page.

If only the word for orange
Sounded as round and juicy
as the one I just ate; If only 'sugar'
did not taste of ashes and chains on black lips,
if only your smile did not leave me speechless
with delight, and Howl
did not rhyme with bowel
and it was enough to spell
tintinnabulation
to be summoned by bells.....

En ce cas, mon semblable
there would be no need for poems
to build bridges of air
    between their words and the world,
as if territory was map
    and map territory........
no need of proofs
for the writing to become fair copy, no call
for punctuation to reach a conclusion,
no justification for end rhymes to underline
the scansion of the text......

Just the slow imprint
of words on deeds, speaking volumes
of a story waiting to be unearthed:
another book as yet unread, pages open
in welcome to the sheltering sky.

TWO: BIRTHPLACES

Of course, thanks to the house, a great many of our memories are housed, and if the house is a bit elaborate, if it has a cellar and a garret, nooks and corridors, our memories have refuges that are all the more clearly delineated. All our lives we come back to them in our daydreams.

- Gaston Bachelard, The Poetics of Space

Home alone

A long corridor, with many doors. It is quiet and warm. There is no one to be seen. The baby sits up in his pram and looks around. He realises for the first time that he exists for himself, and is alone in the world. He does not cry for his mother. He likes it there.

Siren calls

The baby wakes up out of a bad dream. He is being attacked again. The wolf has disappeared but not his howl. It is the siren calling him to prayer. He is picked up and carried downstairs. He can smell the fear and feel it in the arms that hold him. No one talks. Everyone is listening out. At first there is silence. That only means the Thing has not happened yet. If he could have put the Thing into words, it would be saying ' keep your ears skinned and remember, if you fall asleep, I might pounce and you might wake up dead'. Then he hears it, the big whine that only stops when the Thing falls silently out of the sky. He tries to block the world out. He knows the only safe place to hide is in the cave inside his body. He still hears the explosion when it comes. That does not mean it is over. There may be another one. Until the siren says it is safe to come out now. Is there anyone else alive? Will the wolf be back for his supper?

Cold comfort farm

The room is cold. The floor is made of stone. The walls are damp. There is an oven set in the fireplace but the fire is not lit. The old woman he has learnt to call Gan is cleaning the oven. She smells of cold and damp and the stuff she is using to polish the grate. The baby watches from his cot. He longs for the warmth, but knows it will never come from her.

Birthday suit

The baby wakes from a nightmare. To escape from the wolves he runs into a brightly lit room full of people. They turn to look at him and laugh, he does not know why. He jumps onto his mother's lap. She stiffens and freezes. He knows she is angry but he does not know she is embarrassed about being seen to have a naked baby in her arms. Maybe she is also terrified he may one day grow up into a wolf.

Bedtime story

'If you don't go to sleep Wee Willie Winkie will come and get you'. I stay awake, watching out for him, determined he won't get me this time. But he doesn't come, and so, reassured, I fall asleep. Then in my dream he comes, with his red pointed cap, with his pointed nose and ears, with his long fingernails ready to scratch my eyes out. I wake up, terrified, and look around me, but he has disappeared. I am too frightened to go back to sleep in case he is waiting for me there.

Oceanic feeling

A cloud hovers over us, marking our place in an azure sky. The river shimmies past and our boat rocks gently as it moves slowly down the narrow channel. Ahead of us a water rat scurries into the reeds looking as if he is walking on water. My hand makes a little eddy in the current. Then suddenly there is no more cloud, river, boat, reeds, hand. Only the world at one with itself and its witness.

Sofa ahoy

It has a secret lever that you press when you want to turn it into a pirate ship. One end folds down with a drawn out satisfying creak, to make a gang plank allowing passengers to come aboard and mutineers to be thrown to the sharks. When the weather is bad, this is pulled up to make the ship storm proof. The captain's favourite activity on deck is jumping up and down in time to the waves.

Utility chairs[1]

The fact that chairs have four legs rather than two makes them more reliable playmates than children. They might occasionally hurt you or trip you up, but if you kick them, they never kick back. On the whole they do what they are told without complaining. Left to their own devices, they just stand around waiting to be climbed and sat upon, like vacant laps.

We have a set of four wooden 'Utility' chairs and I make sure they live up to their name as I train them to perform all kinds of stunts. The fact that they have lost their arms as part of the war effort, far from crippling their ability to play, makes them even more adaptable for my purposes.

Upright, and placed in two rows, knee to knee, with cushions spread across, they make a comfortable houseboat. Kneeling down facing each other with their

---

[1] Utility furniture was made under government regulation during the war, and was designed to be sturdy and functional, using the minimum of material.

curved backs arched together, they form a splendid tunnel or cave. A single chair, lying on its back, instantly converts into a toboggan, rocking to and fro as I use its legs to steer down a mountainside. Two chairs lying cradled one on top of the other create the cockpit of a Spitfire, or when it is too windy to fly, a submarine.

Then one day some new chairs arrive, huge heavy things with bony arms, straight backs and padded seats, more comfortable to sit on, of course, but completely useless for my adventures. This coincides with our heavy blackout curtains giving way to ones made out of more colourful, flimsy material. In this fashion I learn that the war is finally over.

Under the concrete, the beach

If there was a fire in our flats you were supposed to assemble on the concrete roof. There never were any fire drills, and no-one except us ever went up there. But it served as our garden and our beach. In the summer we used to take a rug and have a picnic or sunbathe. Seagulls would bring the seaside with them as they swooped around us, ready to catch the scraps of food we threw. On a clear day you could see across the whole of North London to Alexandra Palace and beyond. After lunch there would be games. A series of large pipes made good hurdles to jump over and the lift house wall was useful for throwing a ball against. The fact of being so close to a precipice - even if one guarded by railings - gave these family outings a spice of adventure that visits to the park never had.

Home alone: the sequel

Outside our front window there was a small ledge which ran along the whole length of the building and provided a perfect perch for passing pigeons, gulls, and sparrows, much to my delight and my mother's disgust. I wanted her to put bread out for them in winter, but she regarded these birds as pests and refused to do anything to encourage them. Usually the windows were kept shut to keep out the noise and fumes from the traffic. But when the weather was hot they would be opened and once a sparrow seized the opportunity to take up temporary residence, sending my mother into hysterics before it flew out again.

My own favourite perch in the flat was the windowsill which was just wide enough to sit on. If there was no bird life about, I liked to watch the tiny figures of people coming and going in the alleyway opposite. One day, when I was about five, my parents went out to do some shopping, leaving me for the first time alone in the flat. This was the opportunity I had been waiting for to feed the birds. I put some bread out on the ledge, and waited but there were no takers. So what to do next? I had been fascinated by some newsreel pictures I had seen of a ticker tape parade in New York, so now I decided to improvise my own version. I got hold of some old copies of the 'News Chronicle', cut the pages neatly into strips, then used rubber bands and Plasticine to fasten these together and make a kind of paper flying bomb. I leaned out as far as I dared over the ledge to launch my missiles and watched fascinated as they plummeted down into the street, tails streaming behind them; one of them was blown into the alleyway, landing at the feet of an elderly gentlemen out walking his dog, who thought his master was being attacked and promptly tore it to pieces. Exhilarated by my success, I looked around for other ideas. There was a bowl of toffees on the window sill, so these were next to go - how delighted passers-by would be when it suddenly started to rain butterscotch on them out of a clear blue sky....

I was looking around for further ammunition when my game was interrupted by a frantic banging on the door. I immediately thought it must be the head porter who had come to see what was up. But it turned out to be my panic stricken parents who had left the keys inside the flat, having locked the door as a precaution and couldn't remember where they had left them. I tried looking for them following their instructions, but found nothing. Now it was my turn to feel frightened. They couldn't get in and I couldn't get out. What should we do? Call the fire brigade? Get someone to come and knock the door down? Then we remembered the outside window ledge. It was just wide enough for someone to crawl along....

At this point in the story there are three possible endings. The headlines might read ' Young father falls to death trying to rescue son'. No, that is too horrible to contemplate. It did not happen. Or 'Child crawls to safety in rooftop drama'. That was my preferred version to tell to friends. Or, 'Local doctor risks life and limb to find flat keys', which is, in fact, what happened.

As a result of this episode my parents never again left me alone in the flat until I was old enough to be trusted with my own set of keys. A lock was put on the front windows which were never opened, even on the hottest days. Meanwhile I retreated to my bedroom, which looked out on the back of the flats; from this vantage point, whenever I was in the mood and there was no-one about down below, I would lob stuff out the window - oranges, light bulbs, large potatoes - for the pleasure of seeing and hearing things smash to smithereens on the concrete. By these simple means I finally got my revenge on the V2s.

Vice versa

It was to be a grand occasion – a fancy dress party in honour of my friend Robert's eighth birthday held at the Dorchester hotel in Mayfair. And it was indeed a most distinguished gathering: Emperors, Kings, Princes, Generals, a few Cowboys and Indian Chiefs. The girls were mostly Queens, Princesses, or Ballerinas. Robert went as Captain Hook. When I visited the costumier I had toyed with the idea of a piratical outfit, but didn't fancy wearing an eye patch so I settled for being an

Admiral instead. My uniform consisted of a heavy navy blue overcoat with brass buttons and 'gold' braided epaulets with trousers to match, plus a cocked hat with even more gold trimmings. 'A real little Lord Nelson' my mother said.

At first the party went well, although the hat was uncomfortable and the coat not exactly made for romping about. But then I had to go to the 'men's rest room', as it was called. Unfortunately it did not live up to its name. I had no sooner got into a cubicle when a group of boys burst into the toilet and started banging on my door. They eventually left but I was too upset to continue with my business. I rejoined the party, doing my best to carry on as normal. But I dared not risk a return to the 'rest room' and so spent the next two hours in agony, desperately trying not to go in my pants. One of the adult helpers noticed that I looked unhappy and asked what was the matter, but I felt it was beneath my dignity as an admiral to confess the truth. This experience taught me two important lessons for the future: always go to the toilet before you go to a party, and don't expect Kings and Princes to behave any better than eight year old boys. And vice versa.

Growing pains

In each flat there was a small cubbyhole next to the door, where you would put your rubbish to be collected. If we were locked out of the flat, the porter would come and open the cubby door, and I would have to squirm through to let my parents in. But then, one day, when I was about twelve, I went in as usual, head first and found that I just got stuck. No matter how hard I squirmed and my dad pushed I just could not get the rest of my body through. I had banged my head against the cubby roof, my shoulder was hurting, and visions of amputation swum before my eyes, but then I realised with a sudden jolt of relief that I had simply became too big for the job. From this experience I learnt there were some things children could do that adults valued because they couldn't, but there were even more advantages to be gained from growing up.

THREE: LIKE AS NOT – excerpts from Arnold K's memoir

Many thought processes appear to be based on consciously false assumptions, which either contradict reality, or are even contradictory in themselves. But they are intentionally thus formed in order to overcome difficulties of thought, and reach the goal of thought by roundabout ways. These artificial constructs are called scientific fictions, and distinguished, as conscious creations, by their 'as if' character

> *- Hans Vaihinger*

Editor's Introduction

What follows is a selection from the memoirs of Arnold K, a sometime brick maker and monument curator who died in the mysterious circumstances of a sea tragedy. The author referred to this work as his 'scientific fictions', and they were found amongst his personal effects at the time of his death.

K was employed for a time at the Ministry of Public Archaeology, where he was a conscientious worker, well regarded by his peers. It goes without saying that if we rescue his work from the obscurity of the archive, it is not out of any regard for his posterity; nor, it must be said, primarily on account of any literary merit the memoirs themselves may hold. Rather the interest of these pieces lies in the evidence they offer as to the political conditions and social customs of the recent past.

The reader may feel that from an artistic point of view these fragments possess a certain charm but beyond that, even a cursory reading indicates that the inflated claims made on their behalf in some literary circles cannot be sustained. In its frankly tendentious nature, blurring as it does the boundaries between fact and fiction, the work is very much a product of the fashion for mixing genres which was so symptomatic of the cultural instability that marked the transitional period.

The memoirs were found in K's deposit box at the National Digibank. The manuscript was in a very considerable state of disarray. Much of the text was indecipherable due to poor handwriting and numerous corrections. Indeed in places it resembled an ancient palimpsest rather more than a contemporary work! Many of the pieces were unfinished; in some cases they contained defamatory statements, or descriptions of intimate relations which rendered them unsuitable for publication. Of the writings that remained I have selected those which, in my opinion, best illuminate the author's life and times.

Portrait of the author as a child

Little is known of the author's early life, with the exception of a painting reproduced here of him aged about six which was done by his mother, a gifted amateur painter, shortly before her death (see illustration above). His own account of his childhood, in so far as it can be checked against the facts in his file, is a mixture of pure phantasy and wild exaggeration.

I have resisted the temptation to correct inaccuracies of detail and interpretation, as well as infelicities of language. And this for two reasons. Firstly because they bear witness to the author's character and state of mind, and as such corroborate the findings of the expert reports; secondly because I am confident readers will already possess sufficient information about the true course of events from other, more accurate, sources, and so be able to judge for themselves the exaggerated nature of their representation in this text. I have therefore confined my editorial intervention to adding a few supplementary notes to clarify those passages where references may be obscure for those unacquainted with the incidents they describe.

The pages of the manuscript as found were not numbered, nor were the sections dated, and their provenance could not, of course, be established from a computer log. The memoirs were written over a period of several years, and we have been able to establish, thanks to the help of a handwriting expert, the rough order in which they were produced. Unfortunately this in no way corresponds to the order of the events they describe, a fact which bears witness to the author's lack of formal training in the craft of autobiography. I have therefore assembled the pieces according to their objective chronology, following the sequence of life/historical events they record. This task has been made easier by the fact that most (though not all) of the events could be corroborated from independent sources - historical archives, psychiatric and police reports, institutional records, newspapers, and eyewitness accounts. Two such documents are included in an appendix.

There remained however a difficulty with a few of the longer pieces, which comprise an extended narrative containing numerous digressions on the author's philosophy of life. I pondered for a long time as to whether or not to include these pieces. But the fact that they throw light on an obscure chapter in the history of ideas, as well as giving us some insight into the workings of K's mind, persuaded me that they should be retained. Since it is not at all clear where the pieces fit in the sequence, I have placed them where they do the least 'harm' in the sense of interrupting the unfolding logic of the story. Also included here is a personal testimony by an 'illegal' who was a close friend of K's, and which gives us an outsider's view of the civil commotion that preceded our present era of calm and prosperity.

K was an enthusiastic amateur photographer and left behind a collection of some six hundred prints, documenting both public and personal moments over a thirty year period. I have included a few examples of this material where it serves to amplify the text. The titles are his.

Baptismal Naming

They have asked me to write the story of my early years, as if somehow that would explain what has happened to me since. At first I resisted on the grounds that it was an invasion of privacy but then I realised that such a childhood as they wanted was in any case public property, given that so much of it had been spent being observed from behind one-way mirrors. I would risk nothing by complying with their request, and might even gain some advantage. Only later, once I had completed the task to their satisfaction, did I realise that unwittingly I had opened a door into another world that I could not close.

My mother, who was already in her late fifties when I was conceived, became crippled with arthritis shortly after I was born. As a result she was quite unable to hold or feed me. A special prosthetic cradle had to be constructed for her to use with me. I do not have any distinct impressions of it, of course, but I saw one many years later in the Museum of Motherhood. The device had a built in breast made out of synthetic rubber with a large teat that used to play a tune when sucked. I was later told that the model my mother used played Beethoven's *Für Elise*, one reason no doubt why I have always detested his music. At any rate when I was seven my mother died and I was moved to the Centre for the Protection of Abandoned Children. As a keepsake I was given a small toy rocking horse, carved out of wood and painted in bright colours. It had a little door in its belly and inside were lots of little tiny soldiers. You wound it up and it would rock back and forth, back and forth making a soft neighing sound, until you felt giddy just watching it and thinking how sick the soldiers must feel in its tummy. My little horse had been brought back by my great grandfather from his travels in the East and it now became my most treasured possession. If I was miserable or couldn't get to sleep because of the bullies in my head I would roll it back and forth, back and forth until I became mesmerised and fell asleep.

Rock-a-bye baby

My mother once told me its story. Genghis Khan was besieging the Persian city of Hormuz, but could make no impression against the fortress and its courageous inhabitants. So he had a giant horse made and left it outside the gates of the city and then rode away into the night with all his men so the defenders would think he had given up and left it behind as a gift; rejoicing at their delivery, the Persians, the little sillies, dragged the horse within the city walls, and thinking all was well, went off to party and celebrate their famous victory. The horse, left to its own devices, promptly gave birth to its murderous crew, who opened the city gates and let in the rest of their comrades who had sneaked back under cover of darkness. The Persians were slaughtered in their thousands as they slept in a drunken stupor and the city was annexed to the Mongol empire for many generations. A cult of the horse grew up in the city; it came to represent the superior wisdom of the Great Khan and thousands of little models were made so that people could worship him in the privacy of their own homes. Today in parts of our own Empire, some of the descendants of the Khan have taken to erecting monuments to his memory . The moral of the story, my mother said, was that you should never accept a present from anyone who had done you a bad deed, no matter how much they said they wanted to make amends. 'Once an enemy always an enemy' was her unforgiving motto and one that has stood me in good stead.

My parents separated a year after I was born. My father was a famous surgeon who worked in another town. He visited me only once, shortly before Mother died. I was very impressed by the fact he could hold his breath for what seemed like ever, whilst waggling his ears at the same time, a feat I have spent most of my life attempting to emulate, with little success. When, much later, the other children in the centre asked me what Father did, I used to tell them 'he's a knife man, throats slit to order - he gets up people's noses the way a weasel goes after a rat'. They left me alone after that!

When I was about ten, I caught pneumonia and had to be put in an oxygen tent. One day I got a visit from a man I'd never seen before but who somehow looked familiar. He was dressed all in black: black hat, black face, shades, black T shirt, pants, shoes; even his hanky was black. He said his name was BiG Man and that Father was dead, stabbed in the back by a Red. He had heard I was a chip off the old block and handy with a knife. Did I want dad's job as ear nose and throat man to the mob ? As he spoke he clicked his fingers in rhythm to the words, and then I knew where I'd seen him, he belonged to a famous gangsta rap group called Pappa Hemingway.

When I got better, I looked the job up in the dictionary. See under oto-rhino-laryngology, it said. So I did and to my astonishment there was a picture of Father. But even more I was entranced by the music of the words themselves. Oto-rhino-laryngology became my nightly orinasal prayer. Muttered under the breath, over and over again it kept the bogeymen at bay. Shouted out loud it scared Wee Willie Winkie away.

So I started out on a new career as a hard-nosed, thick-skinned, word-gargling rapper, answering to the name of Doctor John. I suppose it made me feel special, being the only one in the Centre to have been adopted by a family of gangsters. When things got difficult for me I waited for BiG Man to ride to the rescue and carry me off on his Ford Mustang. But he never came. I did use to get postcards from time to time saying he was busy running guns to the rebels of the Sierra Madre or killing orang-utangs in Matabeleland.

When the teachers and social workers asked me in their bright, strangled voices where did I get all these strange ideas from, I would reply, quite truthfully, 'from other people'. Later, swapping make believe lives with the other children, I read the same desperado plot between many of their stormy story lines.

When I got to my fourteenth birthday, the counsellors said it was time to give up BiG Man and start doing some growing up myself. I was given some pills that stopped me twitching and rushing about but I still had BiGMan's voice inside my head like a secret digigram telling me to run away and join his rebel army. So when the warden asked me to do the washing up I used to reply, ever so politely, 'I'm sorry, I'm too busy inventing a new kind of oto-rhino-laryngo-technology to get my hands soapy right now'. When the shrink wanted to know about my dreams I would say 'I can't remember them but it's all written down somewhere in my oto-rhino-laryngo-discography' (chanted to a beat she couldn't tap her pencil to). When I ran into the local lads, drunk on moonbeam whisky and spoiling for a fight, I would dial up 666 and whisper otorhinolaryngoscopy over and over down the line till their digiphones were singing like cicadas and the whole gang fell into a trance, and I could leg it back home to safety.

This was how I spent my early years, listening to the rhythm of words and the silences in between.

Trade Mark

In the reformatory they used to call me 'the vulture'. It may have been on account of my beaky nose and hunched shoulders, or the fact that I would sit for hours perched on a wall watching the other boys play football in the exercise yard, and only jump down and join in when the game was nearly over. They used to say I only joined the team I knew was going to win and that the other side would lose heart.

It was my introduction to a principle I have since come to understand as regulating much of our life - that when people act as if something were true then it tends to become so.

When I was 16 I was sent to the Boys' Labour Colony where they taught us manual trades.

The Boys' Labour Colony (author front row, second from the right).

It was the time when everyone was supposed to contribute to the rebuilding of the country after the war. In my case it was decided I should learn how to make bricks that would be used to build houses for those made homeless in the bombing of our capital city. I was sent south with two others to a boys' labour colony situated in the middle of a desolate marshland. There were few roads and no railway and so little possibility of escape. We lived in barracks and were marched every day to the brickfields where we learnt how to mould, set, fire and cool the bricks. The instructor was a dour southerner with an enormous stomach which he used to great effect for pushing the boys around. If he thought you were slacking, or your work was no good, he would hit you with the back of his hand. He delighted in humiliating new boys by sending them on fools' errands. On my second day I was made to climb to the top of an oak tree in search of a 'knobstick' which he claimed was needed to rake the hot bricks out of the kiln. Most of us hated him but he did have his favourites who got better treatment. He would take them off to a 'hide' in the middle of the Nature Reserve for what he described as a bit of extra training. We never discovered what he did with them there, and the boys themselves never told us, but we suspected it did not have much to do with brick making. His favourites were never short of cigarettes or chocolate, while the rest of us had to make do with porridge, bread and potatoes.

After about a year I passed my novice's test and was sent out on licence as a trainee to work in brickfields south of the capital. The work was hard, and involved preparing the clay, cleaning the kilns and stacking the bricks ready for transportation by lorry to the city. 'Novvy labour' the skilled men called it. We 'novvies' lived in dormitories, much like in the reformatory, except we each had our own cubicle. Then an order came to increase production. It seems the government had decreed that a Great Wall should be built to protect our citizens from the corrupting influence of our neighbours. I was promoted to the production squad and granted my own trade mark, which I was allowed to design. I first drew a brick with a crack down the middle as if it had been broken in two and mended by invisible hands and then a small rocking horse, like the one I had been given by my mother. It was my way of remembering where I had come from.

At the gymnasium they had taught us that once upon a time history was a nightmare only the rich awoke from. Nowadays we interpret the dream of reason according to the government's rules. No one is carried off by wolves in their sleep, no one wakes to find a mermaid's hair on their pillow. No one puts out a saucer of milk in the hope of a visit from leprechauns. Yet as I reached my sixteenth birthday I began to have the most vivid dreams. In one recurrent scene, I am marching down an endless road lined with bricks, millions of them, standing to attention, each bearing my trade mark and waiting to tell its own story. My favourite is yellow sandstone, unglazed, baked in a kiln somewhere near my home town and then sent north with thousands of its comrades to the capital, to build the line that broke the city's heart in two. My brick is chosen to be displayed in the Party Musoleum where it lies in state, inside a plate-glass cabinet where it nestles grittily on a plush red cushion with a caption tied like a medal around its throat: this is the brick that made the wall that built the People's freedom.

And then the glass cage shatters. Reason wakes from its beauty sleep. My brick flies off across the city to find a young man's hand waiting to fling the final stone that puts the last red star to flight. Together we are given a new place of honour in the history books. Chippings are sold like indulgences in the auction houses of New York and London. My trade mark appears on a thousand tourist souvenirs. My brick and I are interviewed in newspapers and TV talk shows. I become expert in interpreting its views on every matter of public comment, from the price of herring to the future of planetary travel. In my home town the new management at the Museum of Bricks puts up a statue to me next to a glass case in which what is left of my partner lies on a red plush cushion with another ribbon of lies tied around its throat: 'This is a brick that helped to build the people's freedom'. So it goes.

In some versions of the dream, somewhere around the corner just out of sight, a small boy, it may be my son, or myself as a child, I can't quite tell, is playing with his building set. Sometimes he places one brick carefully on another to build a bridge from himself to other people; at others he makes walls, or skyscrapers simply to enjoy knocking them down and building something up again from the rubble.

Which of these ways of making history will prevail no-one can tell, either under hypnosis or from consulting the archive.

The Tower of Babel

After serving my time at the Labour Colony, I went on to study to become a brick master at the Institute of Vocational Studies. In addition to perfecting technical skills related to the making and laying of bricks, apprentices are required to write a dissertation in which they describe the philosophical foundations of their trade. This normally takes the form of interrogating the many commentaries on the ancient story of the Tower of Babel that have been made by brick masters over the centuries. It was our chance to add a mite of wisdom to the great House of Knowledge.

The Faculty of Brickmaking

There were two main schools of thought about how the story should be understood. Those who followed Master Dunn argued that it was a parable about the envy those without knowledge in their hands feel for those who can make brick and build cities. The Dunnites point out that the earth never was 'of one language and one speech'. Rather, what happened was that the Mayor of Babel conceived an ambitious scheme of urban renewal, with the tower - an early version of the skyscraper - as its centrepiece. The scale of the plan required brick makers and layers from many different parts of the country to work together on the project. Naturally, they spoke many different dialects and used different names for particular tools and processes. Nevertheless, as the story puts it 'they all had brick for stone and lime had they for mortar'. In other words, underneath these superficial differences of custom and culture, labour itself provided a common language. Seeing this, the city fathers became afraid. For, as the story has it 'the people is one and they all have one language, and now nothing will stop them from achieving what their imagination demands - a city of God where justice rules for all'. So the project was cancelled, and the troops ordered in to disperse the brickies to different parts of the country.

A rival interpretation is put forward by the followers of Master Rihm. According to them, the story is indeed about the foundations of language, or rather the edifice of culture that language makes possible. But it pivots on a contradiction. The plan to build a tower that will defy the laws of gravity and reach the sky symbolizes the desire of human beings to transcend their material and all-too-mortal existence on earth through creating cultural artefacts that survive their own death. Yet this desire is in fact only realisable through material means, laying brick upon brick, in a way that undermines - or as the story has it 'confounds' - the whole project. A building is only as good as the bricks it is made of, and no bricks, however well made, last for ever. The brick master becomes the bearer of this contradiction. He is made into a scapegoat for the vanity of architects, and the hubris of city planners who think they can 'build for eternity'. And that is why, all those years ago, we became social outcasts dispersed to the four corners of the earth, where each guild developed its own distinctive code of practice.

The Tower of Babel

Most of my fellow apprentices confined their thesis to a simple exegesis of these two positions, quoting copiously from the various authorities to demonstrate their command over the corpus of texts. Marks were awarded for presentation. Each rubric of the thesis had to be written in special ink using an ancient formula for mixing ochre with fly agaric. The more I considered the question the more dissatisfied I became with both schools of thought. The Dunnites and Rihmists had clearly got hold of opposite ends of the same wrong brick. But how else to make sense of the story? I spent many sleepless nights wrestling with the problem; when I fell asleep I would have confused dreams of being imprisoned in a huge tower, and being made to run endlessly up and down its spiral staircase seeking a way out, whilst at every window and doorway the leering faces of my teachers and fellow students yelled obscenities at me in a dozen foreign tongues.

It was in this agitated state of mind that I decided one day to visit a second-hand bookshop in the City Arcades that I used to frequent in my youth. There I came across a battered copy of Vaihinger's *The Philosophy of 'As If'*. Vaihinger had been a professor at the Institute before my time, but had left under mysterious circumstances, and no-one now mentioned his name or discussed his work. I read the first pages with mounting excitement. For here, spelled out in a dozen or so neatly connected arguments was a framework, which not only made sense of the Tower of Babel itself but also of the rival interpretations placed upon it.

The author explains that what he calls 'the law of preponderance of means over ends' applies universally, and not only in nature, but to culture as well. He gives countless examples of how human thought in the course of time has gradually lost sight of its practical purpose, and become an end in itself. This leads to the creation of what he calls 'scientific fictions', stories that model reality as if it were some approximation of what we would like it to be. These narratives have a dual function. They enable us to act in and on the real world and to fashion it according to our desires. At the same time they create an imaginary universe which, like as not, is premised on quite false assumptions about how the world behaves, even though it offers us some emotional or spiritual consolation for the fate it inflicts upon us.

In my dissertation I argued that the Tower of Babel was a scientific fiction of this kind. The very materiality of the bricks that built it enabled the tower to serve as a metaphor of human productivity; but, at the same time, the story is a parable about what happens when the productivity of thought becomes divorced from the world of practical affairs and declares itself all-powerful. So we are indeed dealing with a myth about the origins of urban civilisation, but one whose building blocks are no longer in the hands of the brick masters, and instead in those who claim a superior vocation in developing the life of the mind and who set themselves up as map-makers of both the heavens and the earth. I showed in my thesis how the whole of human history could be understood as the struggle between these two tendencies, one represented by those who work with the raw materials of nature, with the elements of earth, air, fire and water, and those who sit in offices and libraries and design empires of the mind. I called my theory Third Space to distinguish my standpoint from those who looked at a city and merely saw bricks and mortar, whom I called the 'First Spacers', and those others, the 'Second

Spacers', who regarded all such edifices as the expression of a master plan dreamt up by the Divine Architect and implemented by His representatives on earth.

Inevitably my argument caused a furore at the Institute. Dunnites and Rihmists closed ranks to a man in denouncing me as an apostate. Slogans appeared on the walls: 'Down with Third Spaceism!', 'Kill all Third Spacers', 'There is no Third Space'. My fellow students shunned me, and one day when I went to my locker I saw someone had chiselled the sign of a toad on the door, which in our trade means that you are a marked man and can expect the worst. Even my friends did not want to be seen in my company in case they were taken for 'Third Spacers'. One of them, however, told me that she had overheard some of the students talking in the refectory and how they meant to do me harm.

The staff were, if anything, even more angry. The new Professor of Manual Labour used his inaugural lecture to attack my thesis, which he read as an attempt to undermine the very foundations of his discipline. The Institute authorities called a special meeting of the faculty, and using a technicality (I had not used the correct inks in setting out my rubrics) demanded that I withdraw and rewrite the whole dissertation. When I refused I was summoned to appear before the Council of Artisans to explain myself. I wrote to the Dean, re-iterating my argument and requesting a Public Disputation at which I could defend my views before the whole body of staff and students. In reply I received a letter informing me my apprenticeship had been terminated on the grounds that I was bringing the Institute into public disrepute.

I reacted with indifference. I was already elsewhere. For I had discovered in a single book the key to many things that had long perplexed me.

The City of Déjà Vu

Hans Vaihinger

Not long after this I came across a copy of the controversial paper Vaihinger had written before his dismissal from the Institute. In 'Reflections on Some Foundational Questions in the Narrative Sciences' he argues that the attempt to codify different language uses and correlate them with distinctive speech communities was doomed to failure. Moreover it would only reinforce the worst features of current linguistic practice and the social divisions on which they rested. On the one hand we would have a language of command that was impersonal and devoid of consequential agency, dominated by intransitive or passive constructions in a way that concealed the real sources of power. Authority without authors, he called it. As an example of this device he quotes the usage of the phrase 'it goes without saying' to legitimate any and every remark or opinion. At the same time the paper argues that we would see the emergence of a popular vernacular saturated with stereotypical and abbreviated features so that it was quite incapable of conveying any originality or depth of thought and feeling. He called this the 'wuzzup' tendency. As an example of the alienation this induces, he cites the derisory usage of 'as if' by members of the underclass to express a state of chronic disbelief vis-à-vis promises made by the government to better their lot. The paper concludes that the outcome of the present policy would be to promote civil strife.

This work brilliantly anticipates the fracturing of our culture that occurred at the end of the transitional period when the protocols for knowgov and soapspeak were first established. Indeed the paper is so prophetic that it is easy to see how Vainhinger's enemies in the Institute (and there must have been many who were jealous of his prestige and popularity with the students) could exploit the fact to insinuate that he must have had a direct hand in bringing about events that so closely conformed to his own prognostications. Who can forget Black Saturday and the tens of thousands of young people marching towards the police lines chanting 'As - If, As - If,' whilst tearing up the government's five point programme, carpeting the streets in a storm of white confetti soon to be turned crimson with their blood?

I determined to seek out the author of this famous tract and after making numerous enquiries discovered he was living in a provincial city in the borderlands of our country. I learned from the guidebook that Heliotropolis had been designed by a famous planner of the neo-cubist school to demonstrate the principles of counter-intuitive urbanism.

The layout of the town was designed to provoke a systematic disordering of normal 'lines of desire'. It was no good for example expecting your house to be where you'd left it in the morning when you returned at nightfall. You had both moved on in spacetime and it was necessary to use a new, previously agreed, homing device to ensure you once more coincided with your dwelling place. Equally streets that you thought of as being busy thoroughfares or shopping malls might change into residential cul-de-sacs once you set out on your journey there unless you took account of topical conditions and instead of merely following your habitual route, went with the flow of traffic in the direction of your chosen goal. It was quite usual to experience having been somewhere before even though you knew it was the first time you had ever set foot in that particular neighbourhood, or to come back to where you first started after you had set out to leave the place behind. In all these circumstances you had to act as if none of this were the case, and you could mostly rely on arriving at some approximation of your original destination. Perhaps not surprisingly the citizens of Heliotropolis had developed a horror of the déjà vu, but this took on a particularly acute form related to its peculiar topography.

Heliotropolis

The city was unusual in that it was traversed by three rivers which met in the centre, creating a series of small islands linked by seven bridges. It was imperative to keep these bridges in good repair especially during the Spring floods which every year threatened to wash them away. If that happened whole neighbourhoods would be isolated, often for weeks at a time; food had to be ferried to them in gondolas, a hazardous business which resulted in many deaths as the boats were small and unstable and always at risk of capsizing in the strong currents which might sweep both the boatmen and their precious cargo away downstream.

During the summer months a favourite pastime of the inhabitants of Heliotropolis was 'island hopping' and one of the city's leading mathematicians, hoping to encourage interest in his discipline, set them a problem: Was it possible to walk over each of the seven bridges in turn and make the complete circuit without crossing the same bridge twice? They rapidly discovered that it was impossible. Despite the most ingenious methods of pedestrianism, there always came a point where you arrived at a bridge you had previously traversed, or at least imagined you had. Some of the more adventurous spirits tried to reach a solution by building a skateboard track in the shape of a Moebius strip stretching from one side of a bridge to the other, but after several skaters spun off and badly hurt themselves the practice was abandoned. The professor who had devised the problem as a thought experiment went on to found a new school of mathematics devoted to demonstrating why the problem was in principle insoluble and had nothing to do with the terrain in question. In the meantime the authorities came up with their own solution: they diverted the river and demolished three of the bridges. The affair may have helped put Heliotropolis on the intellectual map, but the citizens were so outraged at having been made such fools of that they ran the mathematician out of town. They got their revenge many years later when rising levels of water led to the complete submergence of the old city centre, and the construction of a new floating island on an artificial lagoon connected by cable cars and hovertrolleys to the rest of the metropolis.

In order to establish some principle of order in this otherwise chaotic city, the planners had introduced a rigorous zoning policy: there were exclusion zones for various types of offender, a homeless containment zone on the downtown island, special narcotic enforcement zones where addicts congregated and everyone was made to take drugs, and drug free zones where you could not even smoke a cigarette without risking arrest.

It was therefore with a mixture of curiosity and apprehension that I set out one late Autumn morning to travel to this strange place in search of my mentor. It was still cool, despite being November, and I caught the hovertrolley, hoping to arrive at my destination before the heat became too intense. The flight itself was as uneventful as the dusty wind-scoured terrain we passed over. The desolate and abandoned countryside suited my mood, yet how I longed for the green fields and winding rivers of my childhood, before the Great Drought turned everything brown and the Great Rains created a sea of mud out of the central plain. We soon approached the coast line, and shortly after we had passed over the now derelict port area I caught my first sight of Heliotropolis as it lay spread out on a peninsula. I have to confess that the sight of all those skyscrapers swivelling in perfect synchrony to face towards the sun moved me to tears.

As soon as I arrived I realised why this place might have possessed such an attraction for Vaihinger. Or, alternatively, why the authorities might have thought it such a suitable exile for him. Its outward appearance was indistinguishable from many of our other new cities, but on closer inspection, beneath the superficially rational order of its architecture there was a quite different principle of organisation at work, one which owned more to the logic of spatial juxtaposition to be found in dreams. I made enquiries and soon received confirmation that the master lived in an estate at the top of the town overlooking the cathedral. Following the strategy recommended by the guidebook I therefore proceeded to descend to what should

have been the lowest point of access to my goal and there sure enough was a sign
pointing to his street with the waypoint co-ordinates indicated.

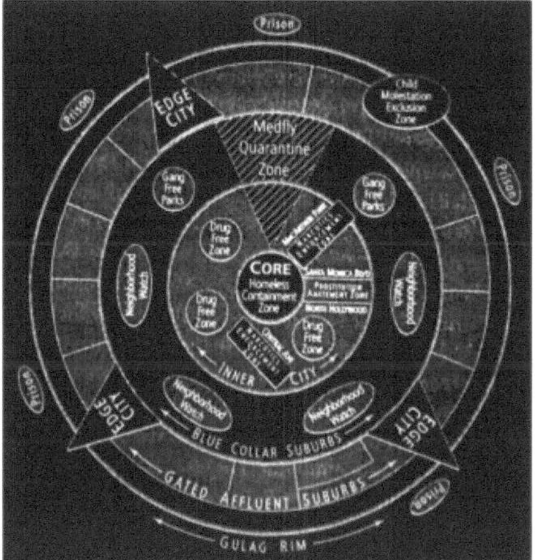

Interzones

In a matter of minutes with the aid of my satnav I had threaded my way
through a maze of narrow alleyways, climbed numerous staircases and dodged past
countless dogs to arrive at an impressive glass tenement which I instantly recognised
as having already been visited in a dream some days previously. I rang the bell and
waited, desperately rehearsing my carefully prepared speech.

The door was opened by a large middle aged woman dressed in overalls.
Whether she was housekeeper, minder, gaoler or nurse, or all four rolled into one,
she was most definitely used to being in charge. She stood there, arms akimbo, feet
planted apart, in a 'they shall not pass' pose. I haltingly explained the purpose of
my visit. She cut me short with an impatient gesture and told me peremptorily that
the Professor did not receive visitors and I should leave immediately. Her attitude
infuriated me. I shouted that I had come a long way to see him and had no intention
of leaving until I could at least reassure myself that he was being properly looked
after. If I was not allowed an interview than she could be sure there would be many
more people like me knocking on the door demanding right of entry.

Whether it was for my spirited protestations or the threat of more visitors,
she suddenly relented and motioned me to follow her indoors. We went down a
narrow corridor and entered a light airy room, with a breathtaking prospect across
the valley to meadows where already Japanese knotweed and barbed goatgrass had
completely overgrown our native species. In one corner by a stove I saw a little
bird-like man with a beard sitting hunched up in a wheelchair, looking away from
me. He was surrounded by books and papers, some in heaps on the floor, some

piled on the table, or spilling onto chairs, and crowding the bookshelves that lined the room.

As there was nowhere to sit, I knelt down next to him, introduced myself and launched into the preamble of my interview. He paid absolutely no attention but started to whistle rather tunelessly under his breath, all the time staring straight ahead of him. I continued but he showed not a flicker of interest in the proceedings. It was like talking to a zombie. I was so agitated by his response, or rather lack of it, that I stood up and knocked over a small vase of flowers on a side table next to me. Again he made not the slightest reaction.

Had he attained that state of transcendence I had spent so long seeking? Or was he simply drugged out of his mind? Or in an advanced state of senility? Had he lost the powers of speech, sight and hearing? Whatever the answer there was clearly no point in going on with the interview. The 'housekeeper' was standing there watching me with an amused 'I told you so' expression on her face. I felt like hitting her.

Then I noticed a display cabinet at the far end of the room which stood out amidst all the clutter. I went closer to inspect it. Inside was a collection of toys, musical boxes, puppets, a model circus with clowns, a seal balancing a ball on its nose. And there right in the middle of the ring, the star of the show, was a little wooden rocking horse, the exact replica of the one I had been given as a child. I rushed over to the case, picked the horse up by its mane and carefully carried it over to Vaihinger. As I knelt down and pressed it into his hands I saw a start of recognition in his face and he smiled. Then he sighed and very gently began rock the horse back and forth, back and forth on his knee, while humming a tune that I dimly recognised from somewhere in my childhood. I suddenly felt dizzy and remember nothing more.

I woke up in hospital. Apparently I had fainted, and the housekeeper, fearing I'd suffered a heart attack, called an ambulance. I had been in a coma for several days but they could find nothing medically wrong with me and after having to undergo various humiliating tests, which involved answering questions a child of five could have managed, I was released.

The Executor

After the Vaihinger fiasco I decided to abandon my studies, but my dispute with the master brickmakers meant it was no longer possible for me to return to my old job. Whether because someone in authority took pity on me, or because it seemed a good way of keeping my mouth shut, I was offered alternative work in the Ministry of Public Archaeology.

The End of History

The Ministry's chief task was to maintain the statues and other monuments to the monarchs, presidents, dictators and other infamous figures who had ruled our country before its liberation. Their presence was an embarrassment to the new regime, which couldn't quite make up its mind what to do with them. They didn't want to destroy the memorials since they served as an object lesson about the past, and might anyway be considered part of the nation's heritage. On the other hand they didn't want them to remain in situ where they might become a rallying point for reactionary or oppositional elements. Or else be vandalised and become an eyesore damaging to the image promoted for the tourist trade. In the end it was decided to remove the monuments to a specially designed 'Park of the Past' located in a remote part of the country, where they could be kept in pristine condition, and access restricted to properly supervised groups of students and foreign visitors.

Entrance to the Park

My job was to photograph and catalogue the statues prior to their removal, recording their provenance and physical condition and making recommendations for their future preservation. Great care had to be taken to calculate the exact treatment required for particular types of stone and metal. It was tedious work but also demanded great attention to detail. By the end of the day I was often exhausted, and suffering from a headache. In order to relax before going home I used to go to a café close by frequented by junior officials from the Ministry. I always ordered the same meal, a plate of potato latkes and chopped liver, followed by a glass of lemon tea. This little ritual gave me something to look forward to in what was otherwise an all too monotonous existence.

We called the café 'Moshe Dayan's', because the owner wore a black patch over his left eye. Whether this was out of homage to the famous Israeli general or because he really was blind, no-one ever dared ask. On this particular day, which was to mark a turning point in my affairs, I entered the café to find two old men sitting in my usual place in the corner by the tropical fish tank. They were presiding over the remains of their meal while engaged in an interminable conversation about the bill, their voices slurred by drink, but still retaining the self-confident ring of people used to being heard in silence. One of them was leaning on a stick, the other clutched a white plastic bag. They were both vaguely familiar, perhaps they too worked at the Ministry and were regular patrons of the café, though I had never noticed them before.

Every so often Stick and Bag seemed to come to an agreement about who was going to pay for what and began to lever themselves up from the table, only to collapse back again into their seats, whether from exhaustion at the effort or because they couldn't bear to break up the party, it was hard to tell. Each time they resumed their places, they started their conversation exactly where they had left off. Their performance reminded me of our national anthem only in reverse - just when you think it is over and can sit down and relax, it starts up again and you have to spring to attention for fear of reprisals.

I tried to concentrate on my meal. Impossible. It was not just their voices, there was something about the quality of their indecision that was infuriating. Only their physical removal from the scene would give me enough peace of mind to eat my food. I called the waiter over and complained that that they were spoiling my meal with their strange antics. 'Just a moment Sir', he replied 'I'll call the boss'. This was the moment I had been waiting for – to see if Moshe Dayan will live up to his name. And how ! He goes straight up to them, seizes Stick by the elbow and Bag by the scruff of his neck, and frog-marches them both out of the cafe. They go quietly, with a meekness that seems slightly contrived, as if to say 'Here we go again, but don't worry, the poor will still inherit the earth. We'll be back to claim at a later date'.

Moshe Dayan comes back with a pleased look on his face, makes a little bow, clears his throat in the manner of a theatre impresario making a front of house announcement about a change of programme: 'Ladies and Gentlemen, the management would like to apologise for the inconvenience caused by these two customers. We have warned them before, they sit here all day and hardly order anything. It's not as if they've got no money to pay for a proper meal. They travel all over Europe, they're well off. One of them buys rare books and manuscripts which he sells to libraries in America, the other translates erotic poetry from Persian and Hindi which he publishes in special editions and sells to private collectors here and abroad. They live together in an apartment in one of the best blocks in town. If you ask me they are perverts. So good riddance to bad rubbish. Now excuse me and please enjoy your meal'. He bows again, and there is a round of applause as he retires behind the counter.

The other diners, who at first had looked rather shocked at the eviction they had just witnessed, were visibly relieved at the explanation. A few shy smiles of congratulation came my way. But now the source of irritation has been removed, I was filled with remorse and had no appetite for my meal. I moved to the corner table. A white plastic bag was lying on the seat. Inside there was a typescript, in a language I did not recognise. My first impulse was to hand the bag over to the café proprietor. But he would probably throw the contents in the dustbin. Perhaps I should run out into the street and try to return it to the unfortunate owners. But maybe it was intentionally left behind in which case I would hardly receive much thanks for my efforts. So should I just leave it for someone else to find? But that is the coward's way out. Besides, I might be in possession of a rare manuscript or a best-selling work of contemporary literature. Perhaps I should show it to a friend of mine who is a literary agent? But then I might be accused of piracy or worse. So what about handing it in to the police? But, there again, suppose it is pornography? I might find myself charged with an offence against public decency and end up in prison.

The more I tried to make up my mind, the more perplexed I became. My head was spinning, my legs went numb, and when I tried to get up to pay my bill and leave I suddenly found I could not move. I tried to signal to the waiter, but my arm was paralysed. It is was if my whole body had turned to stone. Time passes. Most of the other diners have left. Out of the corner of my eye I see Moshe Dayan looking at me curiously. With a superhuman effort, I get to my feet and somehow manage to reach the door. As soon as it closes behind me and I am out in the street I realise with a sickening feeling that I will never be able to go back there again.

Blood Wedding

The doctors had suggested I undertake a daily regime of long walks by the reservoir to restore my spirits. It was on one of these peregrinations that I decided not to return to my job at the Ministry. I had in any case fallen out with the Superintendent of Works over how best to preserve the bronze statuary. I would take early retirement and with my pension travel to other cities, buy a boat, and perhaps even venture across unfamiliar seas to visit my son, whom I had not seen since he was born.

My first expedition was to a city not far away where my daughter lived and which for many years had been divided along religious and political lines. She lived in an area fiercely disloyal to our own government, where the inhabitants wished to be reunited with members of their own faith living in another part of the country. She had married into a family whose members were leading figures in that struggle and now worked as a press officer for a political organisation dedicated to the Cause.

It was an altogether disastrous trip. The long-standing animus between us, which I had hoped my visit would assuage, was only intensified by the political animosity directed against me as a citizen of an occupying power. After a day of rancorous exchanges I left her house to seek lodgings in another part of the city where I might feel more welcome.

My route took me through a cemetery which had appeared many times in the telecasts as a place where the armies of the warring communities came to bury their dead. I came across a group of young men sitting on a bench playing cards. They told me they came there every day, to this particular spot, which marked the exact dividing line between the dead of each side. When the cemetery was first built, it was for everyone. Jews were buried alongside Muslims, Christian graves were tended next to those of atheists, socialist bodies decomposed in soil already made fertile by fascist ones. The final democracy of death. Then, shortly after the outbreak of the Troubles, one of the graves was desecrated, the headstone defaced, obscene drawings sprayed over the photograph of the departed one. No one claimed responsibility, but it was widely believed to be motivated by sectarian hatred. In retaliation other graves were attacked and this continued for many months, until at last it was decided to separate the two communities, and let the dead of each side bury their own dead. One sector was designated for each denomination and a system of trenches and underground walls constructed to prevent any possible intercourse between them. Those who were buried in the wrong place had their bones unceremoniously dug up and re-interred with their own kind. It was in protest against all this that the group of friends, of all faiths and none, met to play cards.

Tombland

Warmed by their story, I resolved to pitch camp right there for the night and began to unpack my things. Outside the gates a crowd of mourners, who had been patiently waiting for the sun to set, suddenly flung their flags up into the sky as if to celebrate my decision. A few of the flags fell billowing around my shoulders, the rest flew off across the now invisible city, making a sign of the cross.

My friends lead me to the chapel of rest, where a guard of honour kneels and fires a discreet salvo of bouquets to waken the other guests. The bride rises and assumes the missionary position, floating above the altar supported by her lover, who is still veiled in khaki. At last she falls into His arms, as if they were not already nailed to the marriage bed.

After consummation, a dance troupe assembles in a marquee to perform the last rites. The bandmaster raises his baton. The audience stand to attention. No-one moves. The musicians too are motionless, unable to utter even the first notes. We hold our breath waiting for the inevitable explosion. Suddenly a cloudburst of champagne beats out a jig on the roof. The guests rush outside, open-mouthed, ready to get drunk on the latest miracle, and start to dance.

Left alone under the wedding table, an old man, who may be my once dead father, or myself in twenty years' time, blows on a battered harmonica, rocking back and forth, back and forth, in silent delight, as if he has suddenly discovered in the music an ancient memory of what it is like to come home after a long war.

Milan's Narrative

Author's Note: One of my colleagues at the Department of Public Archaeology, with whom I became friendly, was an immigrant from one of our overseas territories. I was curious to discover why Milan had undertaken such a hazardous journey to come to a country that was itself so afflicted but my new friend was of a taciturn disposition and reluctant to talk about his past. One day, irritated by my persistent questions, he told me he intended to record everything he wanted to say on the subject at one of the 'listening posts' that the city government had installed in all the main squares, in response to accusations that they were out of touch with public opinion. Nicknamed 'voxpoxboxes' by the soapspeak press, these little booths had originally been used to take photographs required for passports and other official documents. Now they were soundproofed and fitted with a digital video camera activated by inserting one's ID card in the slot provided. In this way every citizen was allowed ten minutes in which to give an airing to their opinions on whatever topic they chose. This exercise in 'digi-democracy' was, the campaign posters assured us, a golden opportunity for the people to tell the government what they thought and wanted.

I encouraged Milan to take this step so that his experience was part of the public record. I thought no more about it. Then one day when I came into work I noticed he wasn't at his desk as usual; he was always punctual and had never missed a day through illness so I immediately knew something was wrong. I asked the director of our section what had happed and he looked surprised. 'What, haven't you heard, it's been on all the newscans - he's dead. He got beaten up by a gang outside one of those grumble booths and died in hospital last night. I can't say I'm surprised. If you ask me he was asking for trouble going there. He should have been grateful we gave him a new start in life, not go about complaining behind people's backs'. I tried to explain that Milan's motivation had been quite different but the director wasn't interested in my theories and waived me away.

I was as shocked by this official attitude of indifference to my friend's fate as I was to the murder itself. But in one sense the director was right. Milan's murder was not unexpected. For a long time immigrants had been the target of such attacks whenever they ventured from their enclaves in the suburbs into the centre of town. Gangs of so called 'wooligans' used to hang around the listening posts and anyone they thought didn't deserve to use them was likely to get roughed up. The government had its own reasons for ignoring these incidents. Still, I couldn't help feeling that I was in part responsible for my friend's death. If I hadn't goaded him with my questions, he would never have put himself at risk. I determined that I would find some way to get hold of his testimony, not only to satisfy my curiosity but so that he need not have died in vain. There would at least be someone who would hear his story. Fortunately I had a contact at the Institute of Narratology who were responsible for archiving and analysing the recordings and she managed to obtain a transcript of Milan's deposition. I have reproduced the text in full below because I want the whole world to know what he suffered.

In tape 31/01 the subject looks straight ahead at the camera, his face impassive for most of the time. His voice wavers up and down, but in regular patterns of stress and intonation which seem intrinsic to the modulation of his national language, rather than to express any individual quirk of utterance or emotion. Every so often, and for no apparent reason, the subject jerks his head up and twists it around to the left as if heading an invisible football. Once, towards the end of his discourse, he smiles.

My name is Milan Andic. It is not my real name, but what I am called now. I am 28 but people say I look older. My wife said I should not do this, these places are traps, so the police can spy on us. But I don't care. My good friend, the one they call 'the vulture', urged me to tell my story, especially because I am not supposed to have one. You can see we always find a way around these problems.

I come from a country a long way away where the government is waging war against our people. They are killing all our young men. They say it is because we are enemies of the state, but we know it is because of our culture and religion. Some of us got out but, whatever happened to our friends and families, whether they are alive or dead, we have all become orphans. I tell the young people they are the future, they must be strong, look out for one another, and not do anything their parents would be ashamed of. But already some of my young friends have become involved with drugs, others go begging or sell their bodies for sex. Everyone attacks them and says they are good for nothing but what else can they do? They have no money, no means of support, the government gives them nothing. There is more than one way to kill the spirit of a nation. To start with you gave us hope but now you are taking it away bit by bit every day, the way a bear strips bark off a tree.

Back home I worked for independence, but I wanted nothing to do with the militias. They are gangsters who just want to become as rich and powerful as our oppressors. I was a journalist, a writer, I spoke my mind, I tried to tell the truth.

So I was a marked man. I heard that the police were looking for me so I decided to go into hiding. I met a man who said he could get me and my family out. It was a long and dangerous journey, but we made it. I am not going to say how.

We came here looking for a safe place, so we could prepare the evening meal without fear of boots at the door. I learnt the native tongue from kitchen porters in the hotel where I worked, so to begin with I could only say fuck to everything. But we lived well from the food I was able to bring out, sides of beef, chickens, cheeses from Italy, wine from France. Then the hotel was raided by police looking for illegals. They found out I did not have a work permit, so I lost the job.

My wife works as a gardener for a rich Jewish woman who is very kind to us. Every day we have fresh flowers on our table. But the room in the hostel is so small there is barely space for our belongings. We have to sleep all together, there is no privacy which means my wife and I could never make love at night as we used to at home. We have to send the two children downstairs to watch TV in the lounge if we want to be alone. If it is the Big Brother or East Enders we can really enjoy ourselves. But sometimes we are not so lucky, the children get bored and we get interrupted. It is hard to judge these things in a foreign country.

My dream is to live in a house by the sea where at dusk only swifts rocket the house tops. I applied for a visa to the United States because I believe such dreams can come true there for ordinary people, not just for the rich. One day a man came from the embassy and told us the papers we had sent had accidentally been lost. I asked him how such a thing could happen. He shrugged and said they had been shredded into ticker tape to celebrate the Dodgers winning the baseball championship in New York. At first we thought he was joking but it seems he wasn't. He was very apologetic, he gave us some more forms to fill in and we paid him some more money. I don't know if it was a bribe or a fee but since then we have heard nothing. Now I am thinking we should complain to the authorities. I am hoping that those who see this tape will do something on our behalf.

They tell us the war is over, it is safe to go back. But every day I read in the newspapers about more killings, more house burnings, more rapes, only now it is our people who are doing these terrible things. This is no longer my country, it is not a place where I want to bring up my children, but what future do they have here? You who are used to taking decisions about other people's lives, what would you do in my place ?

Like as not, the voyage

Like as not the voyage will prove too much for me. It will be my first, and possibly, last adventure on the high seas. Many have warned me against it. The boat is unsuitable, the weather inclement, my health unsure. The omens are not good.

It is not as if I was young, or desired fame and fortune. My decision to rescue the hulk from the municipal scrapyard where, like so many others of its kind, it had been left to rot, was prompted by a sense of affinity with its plight and, I have to admit, a perverse desire to pursue a lost cause......

I had also been struck by the name. Omeros. It sounded like a wave breaking gently on some far off shore. I used to whisper it like a mantra to encourage myself when the going got rough......

The conversion of a canal boat into a sea-going craft posed a constant challenge to both skill and resourcefulness. From the construction of bilge keels out of recycled petrol pumps to the design of wind stabilisers from disused solar panels, the process of refurbishment was one long struggle of human ingenuity against the recalcitrance of things.....

The work was hampered by the fact my back had given out. It was as if I was wired to an electric cactus lodged in my spine that sent great shocks of pain down my legs every time I moved. A hundred times a day, as I levered myself up and down the companion way, crawled along the deck, or clambered around the cockpit, Lady Sciatica led me on her merry dance. The only relief was to sit or stand absolutely motionless, whilst breathing as slightly as possible, until the agony subsided......

I knew I was a figure of fun for the local inhabitants. A batty old man living on a derelict barge, beached in a car park and surrounded by curious shoppers. Mostly people left me alone, but there were always a few wooligans who tried their luck. I gave one of them a scare one night as the youth tried to empty a bucket of piss into the foc'sle, I didn't have any more trouble from them after that.......

After the day's work was done I would go up onto the bridge, which doubled as my study, slip a packet of frozen peas down the back of my pants to ease the pain, and settle myself down in my armchair to work on my memoirs. I would often write until the sky began to lighten, soothed by the sound of cicadas lapping against the hull of the boat and the sense of being in absolute command of my destiny.

Then if I still had some energy left, I would go down to the darkroom I had built and print up some pictures........

Now that I had cut all terrestrial ties, I at last began to feel less encumbered by my past. Yet on my few trips to the supermarket I had the familiar uneasy feeling I was being watched, or, worse, followed, as if a ghost was stalking me still.........

One night I had a dream of being blindfolded and led out by invisible hands onto a great square in the middle of a deserted city. An airship that resembled my boat hovered overhead, with a rope ladder dangling down ready for me to climb aboard. I longed to do so, but could not move for fear of awakening the pain in my back. I thought about making a sudden lunge for the rope, but before I could make the attempt, the airship suddenly exploded into a giant ball of green, gold and orange smoke that assumed the form of Garuda ....

I woke up with an agonising cramp in my leg, but knowing that it was time to make my final preparations. I consulted the on-line almanac to work out the tides, currents and winds needed to carry me along the coast to my destination. I do not trust the official charts. I know the coast from having walked along it as a boy. Having determined the exact nature of propitious circumstances required, I waited for a sign to embark ....

Editor's Note : At this point the writing breaks off. A diary covering the last nine months of K's life was found amongst his personal effects. He used the diary to record both dreams and waking thoughts, including descriptions of his states of mind, and of occurrences in his daily life. Many of the entries are illegible, but we have been able to reconstruct some with the help of the Angloglob Foundation. For the sake of completeness we have reproduced here a sample of the material, drawn from entries covering the final days of his life.

Diary Entries

January 1st

A day like any other for me. I have long lost the habit of mindless celebration which marks our official festivities. At least it is a little cooler today. I made some progress with fixing the steering gear and continue servicing the engine. The manual is useless, having been written for people used to looking for left handed spanners. The pain relented a little after I spent half an hour hanging from the pulpit. Tomorrow I will try to repaint the stern boards.

January 4th

Delivery of rudder and autopilot. Struggle all day to assemble the parts. Completely exhausted by the effort. I have been unable to sleep for the last two nights due to the pain. It is as if I am trapped between two sheets of plate glass, one inside, separating my body and feelings from mind and language, the other between me and the outside world. I am suffocating with rage at my condition and at the same time petrified of letting go of it. The only way out of this state is to make a move behind my own back because otherwise every healthy impulse seems blocked.

January 7th

At last some relief from the unremitting pain of the last few days. It has left me with both legs entirely numb. The absence of pain is actually accompanied by a sense of loss. I am terrified that the slightest movement will aggravate the sciatic nerve and bring the whole agony back. Yet I almost long for the certainty of fate this would bring. Can one become as addicted to pain as to pleasure?

January 12th

A better day. Both the work on the boat and the writing are making progress. Will there come a time when I am finished with both?

I fall asleep early. I dream I am at the city courthouse. There is a ladder screwed to the wall, with a signpost pointing upward ' To Knowledge'. The ladder almost reaches to the ground, but the bottom rung is missing. It leaves a small gap which you can easily jump down to reach the ground, but somehow I don't seem able to do it. At the top of the ladder there is a rope twisted into a noose where a Court Jester or Fool has hung himself. On the ground below two men come out of the courthouse, a law student and myself. We have given up on the case and are on the run from the Moderators. Opposite the building, a bicycle is upside down. The back wheel is missing and the pedals and chain are just racing around out of control.

I wake up realising that the manic panic is back in charge. I fall asleep again then suddenly wake up in terror feeling that my head is becoming completely disconnected from my body and may fall off at any minute. Somehow I manage to pull myself together again with the help of my exercises.

<u>January 16th/17th</u>
I go to the shop but once more have the distinct sensation of being watched. I get into an argument with the till girl because she tries to short change me. The writing is not going well. I fall asleep just before dawn.

Another nightmare. Two masked hoodlums get into my mind. One of them slowly pulls a black balaclava over my face until I can neither see or breathe. Then the phone rings. I try to hold the receiver down on its stand, to prevent myself picking up the message of doom. As I struggle with the receiver it breaks in two. I grab the mouth piece and try to shout for help but there is no one there. In the ear piece I can only hear my own voice screaming. Despite all my efforts I can't put the mouth and ear pieces back together again, the bridge between listening and talking seems irretrievably broken. I wake up feeling completely out of my mind. Thank God the hypnotherapy brings me round in time to receive my visitor.

<u>January 20th</u>
Gondywallahs, chuckyhoops, cruddywuddies and loonyspoons.....once you have discovered the joys of jumbly, the wonders of word gargling, there is nothing much left to say....

Coroner's Report

The circumstances of the client's death are a matter of public record. Following an episode in which he was rescued from his sinking boat off the East Coast, Mr K was committed to St Basil's hospital suffering from acute hypothermia. Shortly after midnight on January 23, he gained entry to the Cryogenic Unit using an ID card stolen from the ward nurse who attended him. The client incarcerated himself in cubicle 4 of the bodybank where, according to the autopsy carried out by Dr Thompson, he died shortly after 2 a.m. His body was discovered the following morning by Ms Swenholt, a contract cleaner. All attempts to revive him failed and he was declared officially dead at 10.23 a.m. The autopsy indicates that death was due to heart failure as a result of acute hypothermia.

The deceased left no will or letter making clear his intentions. From his unpublished memoirs, which I have read, it seems that he had an interest in attaining prolonged states of suspended animation and it cannot be ruled out that he was undertaking an experiment of this kind which misfired. However the weight of evidence suggests a suicidal motive. The psychiatric reports indicate a long history of mental instability and depression. Since leaving his post at the Ministry of Public Archaeology under something of a cloud, it seems Mr K led an increasingly solitary and desperate life. The fact that he set to sea in bad weather in a boat wholly unsuited to these conditions indicates a highly self-destructive disposition; the diary entries written shortly before his death certainly point to the balance of his mind as being disturbed. The further fact that his father, a well-known medical man, was a strong advocate of euthanasia may well have been a crucial factor in the son's decision; in this context the choice of his birthday for the act may not have been coincidental. Taking all these factors into consideration, the court has reached the conclusion that he took his own life.

On 30.01.2043 Mr Archivili Gorki, proprietor of The Nutribox, recorded the following deposition in the presence of the Coroner's Clerk:

He was, how can I say, a bit odd. Not the usual sort of face we get around these parts. A middle aged gentleman, well dressed and obviously well educated, yet fluent in soapspeak, and spending his time hammering nails into that old wooden coffin of a boat of his, moored right there in the middle of the customers' parking lot. When he first arrived, I told him 'this is a car park, not a boatyard, you'll have to move'. But he offered payment, so we let him stay.

Sometimes after a frenzied bout of hammering, he'd suddenly stop, like he'd had a seizure and stand or sit totally still, for maybe half an hour at a time, and always facing north towards Heliotropolis. It looked as if he was praying, though to or for what I couldn't say. He became quite an attraction I can tell you. People used to come from miles around just to see the boat and watch his antics. It was all good for business, of course, so I used to let him have a little discount on what he bought from the shop. It was never much, just the usual nutripacks and toiletries. He used to buy a lot of frozen peas though. I've no idea why. Perhaps he was on a special diet, or it was something to do with his religion.

He also had a hard time with the local wooligans. They called him 'the vulture' on account of his appearance, I suppose. He had hooded eyes, a hooked nose, and always wore black. They used to come along in the middle of the night when he was asleep and piss or pour paint all over the boat. But he caught one of them at it, pulled the lad's trousers down and cut his foreskin off with a razor blade. They stopped after that. It was rumoured he had a gun.

Everyone was a bit scared of him, to tell the truth. Even the authorities left him alone, except that time two detectives came round asking a lot of questions. There wasn't much I could tell them. I never got to know him personally. He never spoke much, but he had a kind of hunted look, as if he was on the run from something or someone. Yes...... definitely there was something deep troubling him, he was always looking over his shoulder. And then, one day, without telling anyone, he just took off, boat and all. No forwarding address. No thank you note. We thought he'd just moved to another site. Then, a few days later, we saw him on the newscan being winched out of the sea.

Now he's dead, we get a lot of visitors asking to see where he lived. Apparently he was a writer of sorts, and had once been famous, though I don't know for what. We're thinking of getting hold of another canal boat, filling it with stuff about him and charging people to visit, or even stay overnight. You never know, we might make enough profit to put up a statue to him one day.

The Boatyard

NOTES

Baptismal Naming

This text was probably written at the instigation of doctors while K was in hospital recovering from his breakdown. It was certainly written much later than the childhood and youth pieces that follow it.

The title refers to the work of an obscure linguist Gyorgy Kripke (1923 - 1987) who argued that the original descriptive name given to an object tends to stick to it even when the object itself changes in character, thus indicating that the signifying function of language always transcends its referential aspect, whilst never entirely becoming independent of it.

Trade mark

The basic facts in this account seem accurate and have been corroborated from independent sources. However his description of the regimes in the reformatory and work camps is not borne out by official reports into conditions obtaining there. See *National Audit of Corrective Work Placements: 25 years of progress,* published by the Moderators Office 2058.

The Tower of Babel

Hans Vaihinger (1889 - 1946) was a minor German philosopher who attempted to reconcile the idealism of Kant with the positivism of Auguste Comte. His main book *The Philosophy of 'As if'* has been seen as a precursor of transcendental materialism, and even of neo-liberal realism. Vaihinger's work is now largely forgotten, but it continues to enjoy an underground reputation in fringe intellectual circles. For a good account of this obscure chapter in the history of ideas see *Dreams and Divagations or 'Vaihinger's Folly'* by Henri Raison (trans. D Nicholson Smith), published by Blitz Books 2018.

For a discussion of the biblical myth of 'The Tower of Babel' and its later appropriations by the Guild of Master Brickmakers see *Building Blocks : the story of the Tower of Babel* by Mansel Dearman, published by the Ministry of Public Archaeology. The author, who was Professor of Manual Labour at the Institute of Vocational Studies at the time K was an apprentice there, veers toward the views of Mikal Rihm, although, for the most part, the treatment is even-handed.

City of Déjà Vu

The guide quoted here is Italo Calvino's *Invisible Cities* (20ᵗʰ edition). For many years this was regarded as a work of fiction, but then detailed plans were found, together with photographs, indicating that some at least of these cities had existed, either as design projects or built environments. Further research carried out by urban archaeologists at the University of Brusel discovered traces of many other cities that did not obey orthodox space/time frameworks. This research is brought together in a great encyclopaedic survey by Schuiten and Peeters *Le Guide des Cités Obscurs* published by Casterman in 2050. The principles of non - Euclidean geometry were further developed by the neo-cubist school of urban design. The famous planner referred to here as the architect of Heliotropolis is probably Eugen Robick. For further information about his work see Schuiten and Peeters, op cit.

The Executor

Moshe Dayan directed the Israeli 'blitzkrieg' offensive during the 6 Day War which laid the foundations for the Greater Jewish Homeland which exists today. 'Doing a Moshe' is a soapspeak phrase used to denote any decisive action. It is probable that 'Moshe Dayan' was a nickname applied to the café proprietor on account of this supposed quality.

There are no means of verifying the events described here. I would however point out that far from being patronised by staff from my ministry, the café in question was a known haunt of dissidents, illegals, and others on the run from the authorities. The owner was well known to be a migrant trafficker and dealer in stolen goods.

Blood Wedding

The title may refer to a play by an obscure Spanish writer from the early part of last century, Federico Garcia Lorca (1898 - 1936). However there seems to be little in common between the two authors apart from a generally rebellious stance towards authority, and just possibly, homosexuality. The frankly delusional nature of this account of a visit to the multi-faith cemetery (since virtualised) confirms the medical diagnosis of K's psychological condition.

Like as not, the voyage

The closure of all inland waterways to both commercial traffic and pleasure craft, and their transformation into reservoirs by the National Water Conservancy Authority, resulted in a large number of boats becoming available for other purposes. Many people converted them into caravans or bought them as second homes, and special public areas were set aside for their relocation. It is typical of K's character that he refused to use these facilities.

Wooligans is a soapspeak term referring to gangs of youth wearing balaclavas who engage in various types of delinquent and anti-social activity. They seem to have made a deep impression on K as witness the dream reported in the diary entry for January 16/17. The term itself is probably derived from 'hooligans' which is itself a corruption of 'Hoooley's Gang', a group of Irish girls who terrorised the neighbourhoods of South London at the end of the 19th century.

IMAGES

1. Untitled - by Stephen Thomson
2. Lewis Carroll's Ocean Chart - reproduced with permission
3. Bitter Sweet - Author's Photograph
4. Storm in a teacup - Author's photograph
5. Mondrian Trees - reproduced with permission
6. Mondrian Trees Abstraction - reproduced with permission
7. Franco Moretti Tree Diagram - reproduced with permission
8. Roots Radical Graffitti - Author's photograph
9. Keep off the Trees - Author's photograph
10. Under the paving stones, the river - Author's photograph
11. Thames Estuary Chart - reproduced with permission
12. Jean McNeil - Sea wall with figures
13. Jean McNeil - Wild Wood
14. Jean McNeil - Autumn Bonfire
15. Jean McNeil - From the Train, Snow
16. Jean McNeil - Spring Trees
17. Jean McNeil - Dazzle
18. Jean McNeil - Passing Storm
19. Jean McNeil - Path to the Woods
20. Jean McNeil - Light Flaw
21. Portrait of the author as a child
22. Rock-a-bye baby - open-source Image
23. The Boys' Labour Colony - reproduced with permission
24. The Faculty of Brickmaking - open-source image
25. The Tower of Babel by M.C.Escher - reproduced with permission
26. Portrait of Hans Vaihinger by an unknown artist - open-source image
27. Heliotropolis - reproduced with permission
28. Interzones - reproduced with permission
29. The End of History - Author's photograph
30. Entrance to the Park - open-source Image
31. Tombland - Author's Photograph
32. The Boat Yard - Author's photograph
33. Jean McNeil and Phil Cohen - photograph by Leslie Bell.

ABOUT THE PUBLISHER

MICA PRESS

www.micapress.co.uk

Other books

In print:

Archipelagos by Leslie Bell

Published 2012. ISBN 978-1-869848-01-9 paperback £8.00

"Leslie Bell's poetry is antic, metaphysical, witty and lugubrious,
traditional and modern, highly literary, and always glancing off in
unexpected directions…He deserves to be read by all who value craft,
daring and sheer exuberant playfulness". John Muckle

Forthcoming:

Recent work by Michael Vince, the poet of *The Orchard Well*,
In The New District, and *Mountain, Epic, Dream*,
winner of the Eric Gregory Award for the pamphlet *Gaining Definition.*

Phil Cohen came to creative writing through the practice of ethnography and through the painting of his partner, Jean McNeil. He has recently published *On the Wrong Track? East London and the Post-Olympics* (Lawrence and Wishart) and a memoir, *Reading Room Only* (Five Leaves). His poems have been published in various literary and cultural magazines, including Agenda, Soundings and Critical Quarterly. *Material Dreams*, a collection of his academic writing is forthcoming from Palgrave, Macmillan. He is Emeritus Professor of Cultural Studies at the University of East London, a Visiting Professor at Birkbeck College and he recently founded Living Maps with John Wallet. Website and blog: www.philcohenworks.com.

Jean McNeil started to paint in her late thirties, studying at the Camden Institute, City Lit (with Cecil Collins) and Hornsey Art School (then Middlesex Poly). For the past two decades she has been inspired by East Anglian land and seascapes and now lives in Wivenhoe near Colchester. She has had solo exhibitions at the Wivenhoe Gallery; Les Livres and Digby Galleries, Colchester; the John Jones Art Centre, Dryden Street, Original and Highgate Galleries, London; and the Smee Gallery, Norfolk. A retrospective exhibition and film about her work is forthcoming in 2015. Her work is in many private collections. Website: www.jean-mcneil.co.uk.

www.ingramcontent.com/pod-product-compliance
Lightning Source LLC
Chambersburg PA
CBHW042111030726
47599CB00002B/183